Coral Reef
COLORING BOOK

Ruth Soffer

Dover Publications, Inc.
New York

Bibliographical Note

Coral Reef Coloring Book is a new work, first published by Dover Publications, Inc., in 1995.

DOVER *Pictorial Archive* SERIES

International Standard Book Number: 0-486-28542-1

Manufactured in the United States of America
Dover Publications, Inc., 31 East 2nd Street, Mineola, N.Y. 11501

PUBLISHER'S NOTE

The brilliant colors of coral reefs—green, purple, orange, red, in a broad range of indescribable shades—may be seen for miles and miles in tropical waters in some parts of the world. These reefs have their basis in living creatures called polyps. Coral polyps (or more simply corals), found only in marine environments, are relatively primitive creatures that attach themselves to the ocean floor in calm, shallow tropical waters. Coral polyps all have a ring of tiny tentacles surrounding a central mouth supported on a stem. Minuscule creatures that swim past are stung and eaten. Some types of corals living in huge colonies secrete a hard substance made of limestone, and this builds up over years to create vast reefs. The varied colors of many coral reefs come from neither the living coral nor their limestone deposits, but from algae—tiny plants that survive inside of the corals, benefiting them and benefiting from them in turn.

The sea, and particularly coral reefs, has a variety of life forms broader than in any region of land. Representatives of these creatures are depicted in the drawings that follow in this book. They are divided among the following *phyla* (plural of *phylum*, the largest subdivision in the animal kingdom).

Porifera. These are the sponges, the most primitive animals after the single-celled protozoa. Sponges are multicellular but the cells are not differentiated into distinct tissues or organs.

Cnidaria (or Coelenterates). Cnidaria are slightly less primitive than the sponges. They may be free-swimming or they may live attached to fixed objects. Cnidaria include jellyfish, sea anemones and corals themselves.

Echinodermata. These creatures of many forms are all protected by hard but often flexible shells or skins. Echinoderms are typically divided into five or more segments, although this is not always obvious. This group includes starfish, sea cucumbers, sea urchins and crinoids (like starfish but with long, thin, wavy arms).

Annelida. These are the segmented worms. Unlike the above phyla, which are found only in the sea, Annelida live everywhere—in fresh water, in saltwater and on land. The earthworm is the most familiar annelid. Many very strange types live in the sea, some anchored to a single spot, others free-swimming.

Arthropoda. There are far more arthropods than any other kind of animal. About ninety percent are insects, and many of the rest are spiders, centipedes, etc., none of which is found in coral reefs. Crustaceans, however, are arthropods that *are* found in coral reefs. These include several species of crabs. Other crustaceans include shrimps and lobsters.

Mollusca. Mollusks are another enormous phylum of animals, found in fresh and salt water and on land. Many have hard shells, but many do not. Snails, octopuses, squid, oysters, mussels and clams are all members of the phylum Mollusca.

Chordata. This large and very varied group includes all of the vertebrates. Chordates are animals with some form of spinal cord (at least at some stage of their development). There are so many chordates that they are divided into many subphyla and classes.

Of those subphyla of chordates represented in this book, that of the Tunicata is the only one that is unfamiliar to most people. Tunicates are small rounded or tubular animals, some types of which fix themselves to the ocean floor or another creature, and then feed on the tiny animals and plants that drift by. Much more primitive than other members of this phylum, tunicates are classified with the chordates because at least in some life stage a simple spinal cord develops in these strange animals.

The other members of the Chordata need little introduction. They include the true vertebrates, animals with developed skeletons: fishes, amphibians, reptiles, birds and mammals. Although most reptiles and mammals live on land, some have adapted to life in the sea and are found around coral reefs. One reptile and one mammal are represented in the drawings in this book.

Of course there is an abundance of fish amid coral reefs. Many are among the most colorful in the world. Don't be afraid to give them lively, shimmering colors in the drawings that follow!

In each of the drawings, the most prominent coral-reef inhabitants depicted are identified by common name and, in most cases, by Latin name.

A number of the drawings are shown in color on the covers, and alphabetical lists of common and of Latin names appear at the back of the book.

The **Blue Devil** (*Abudefduf cyanea*; top) is a brilliant blue fish, popular as an aquarium fish. The **Sea Tulip**, **Ascidian**, **Tunicate** or **Sea Squirt** (right), as it is variously called, is a strange creature (order Ascidiacea of the subphylum Tunicata) that looks like a plant but is an animal, and actually has a primitive backbone in the larval stage. Sea Tulips feed by filtering small creatures from the water. At the bottom are two **Studded Starfish** (phylum Echinodermata). (South Sea, Australia.)

Related to the Seahorse, the strange-looking **Leafy Sea Dragon** (*Phycodurus eques*) is a species of Pipefish that inhabits reefs in the South Sea of Australia.

Here are three varieties of **Nudibranch** (order Nudibranchia) inhabiting Australia's Great Barrier Reef. These brightly colored shell-less snails are mollusks feeding primarily on sea anemones. The Nudibranch at the left (*Jason mirabilis*) is covered with spines. At the top right is the **Spanish Dancer Nudibranch** (*Hexabranchus sanguineus*).

The **Harlequin Tusk Fish** is a sharp-toothed inhabitant of the Great Barrier Reef.

The **Blue-ringed Octopus** (*Hapalochlaena maculosa*) is also a mollusk—
a poisonous member of its family dwelling in Australia's South Sea.

The **Moorish Idol** (*Zanclus canescens*) lives around Australia's Great Barrier Reef. This exotic-looking fish (growing to about eight inches) is a prized—but hard-to-keep—aquarium fish.

Center: **Cherry Blossom Anthius** (*Anthius* sp.). This colorful fish lives in Suruga Bay (Japan). The tentacle-waving **Cerianthid** (phylum Cnidaria) is a nocturnal coral-building creature that looks like and is related to the anemones.

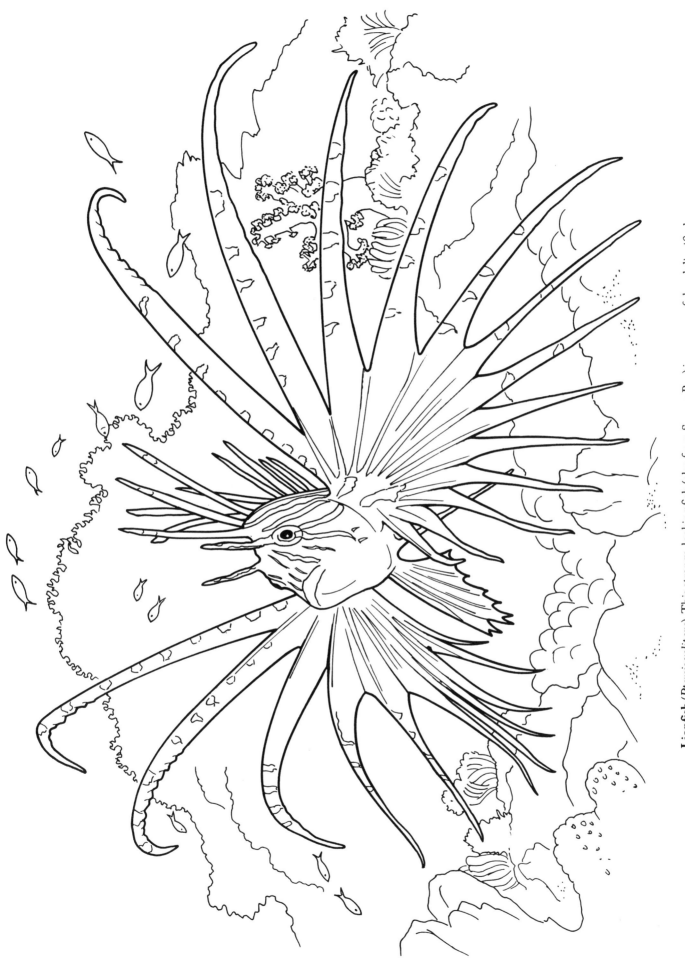

Lionfish (*Pterois volitans*). This strange-looking fish (also from Suruga Bay) is very graceful and dignified in its behavior. Its spines are as fearsome as they look, being highly poisonous. It eats mostly crabs.

Cuttlefish (order Sepioidea). This mollusk is closely related to squids and octopuses (Suruga Bay, Japan).

Spotted Triggerfish (*Balistoides viridescens*). The spots of this triggerfish are not always clearly visible. The sharp teeth of all triggerfish enable them to crush the shells and hard crusts of the creatures they feed on. (Red Sea.)

Royal Empress Angelfish (*Pygoplites diacanthus*). This is a royal-looking fish indeed, its coloring a striking contrast of blues and yellow. It feeds on sponges and algae, among other small items. (Red Sea.)

Foreground: **Red Clownfish** (*Amphiprion frenatus*). Like all clown—or anemone—fishes, the Red Clownfish lives among the poisonous tentacles of sea anemones. The **Three-spot Damselfish** (*Dascyllus trimaculatus*) is one of many damselfish living among corals and feeding on small crustaceans. The **Sea Anemone** (order Actiniaria) itself is a cnidarian, related to corals. It is familiar for its masses of wavy tentacles. (Red Sea.)

Center: **Saddleback Butterflyfish** (*Chaetodon ulietensis*). This black, white and yellow butterflyfish is, like many of its family, popular as an aquarium fish. Upper left: **Snapper** (*Lutjanus* sp.). One of many types of snapper, this fish is common in coral reefs of the Pacific. There are several corals in this drawing. At the left is a **Nephtheid** (family Nephtheidae), a "soft" coral. At the right is **Dendronephthya** (*Dendronephthya* sp.), also a "soft," non-reef-building coral. At the bottom is **Plate Coral** (*Valonia ventricosa*), a "hard" coral. (Great Barrier Reef, Australia.)

On the sea floor is **Star Coral** (*Montastrea cavernosa*). This coral forms mountainous clusters. Above it is a plumelike **Gorgonian** (order Gorgonacea), also a coral, from a group that includes the sea fans and whip corals. The crab at the left is a **Coral Crab** (*Carpilius corallinus*), a very large crustacean with rich red coloring. Finally, there is the **Stone Crab** (*Menippe mercenaria*), a stubby, stonelike red or (when young) purple crab. (Caribbean.)

Bottom: **Elkhorn Coral** (*Acropora palmata*), the most common coral in the Caribbean, forming enormous colonies in shallow waters. Swimming around it is the **Hawksbill Turtle** (*Eretmochelys imbricata*), the only reptile depicted in this book. This shy sea turtle feeds on sponges. (Caribbean.)

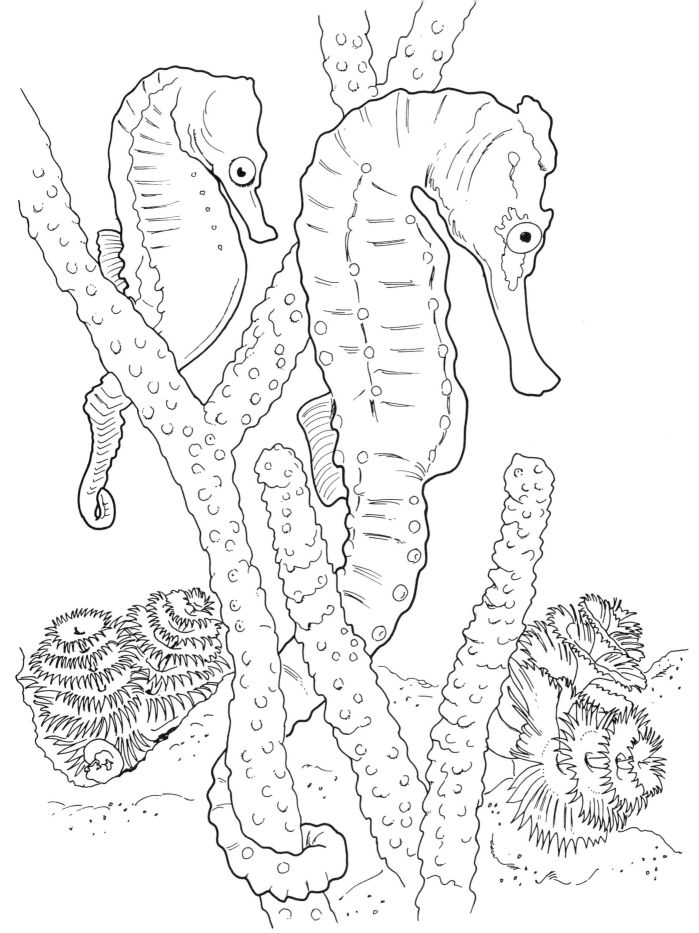

Center: **Seahorse** (*Hippocampus* sp.). This strange small fish is well known from aquariums. It looks like a little horse. It is also unusual in that the male incubates the female's eggs in a pouch. It is wrapped around a **Gorgonian** (order Gorgonacea; see page 17). The **Spiral-gilled Tubeworm** (*Sebellastarte* sp.), bottom, is an annelid. Tubeworms are confined to their tubes, cementlike structures anchored to the ocean floor. They filter food from their surroundings. (Caribbean.)

The coral at the bottom is a **Hydro Coral** (*Stylaster roseus*), a hydrozoan, a special class of reef-building corals. Above is a **Scrawled Filefish** (*Canterbines pullus*), and the large fish in the center is a **Taillight Filefish** (family Melancanthidae). (Caribbean.)

This view of a Caribbean coral reef features three kinds of **Butterflyfish** (family Chaetodontidae). The coral shown is a **Sea Fan** (*Gorgonia* sp.), with broad, branching, fanlike structures.

Above: **Stoplight Parrotfish** (*Sparisoma viride*). This fish gets its name from the female's bright red belly and fins. Males, also beautiful, with shades of blue-green and pink and yellow, look very different. Center: **Princess Parrotfish** (*Scarus taeniopterus*), a lovely multicolored fish, orange, yellow and blue in delicate shades. Behind the fish is **Fire Coral** (order Milleporia). Only distantly related to true corals, fire corals are of a distinct class (Hydrozoa). Brushing against one can cause a painful welt, the tiny polyp colonies injecting poison into the skin. (Caribbean.)

Top: **Nassau Grouper** (*Epinephelus striatus*). This fish—unusual even for a Grouper—passes through up to eight color phases with all sorts of different patterns, sometimes all in a few minutes! Below is a **Yellowmouth Grouper** (*Mycteroperca interstitialis*), a little-known, handsome grouper. Growing on the ocean floor is a **Callyspongia Sponge** (*Callyspongia sp.*) (Caribbean).

The **Frogfish** (*Antennarius* sp.) is a type of angler fish, and a voracious feeder. Its appearance is bizarre but sometimes strangely beautiful. Bottom: the **Atlantic Purple Sea Urchin** (*Arbacia punctulata*) is an echinoderm, related to starfish. It is a spiny creature that lives on the bottom of the sea. (Caribbean.)

The **Spanish Hogfish** (*Bodianus rufus*). When small, this lovely yellow and brownish red fish eats parasites from the bodies of other fish. Later it switches to tough food such as crabs and sea urchins. Below it are two common starfish called the **Thorny Sea Star** (*Echinaster sentus*). (Caribbean.)

The mountainous coral at the bottom is a form of **Star Coral** (*Favia fragum*), a yellow or brownish white coral that forms small colonies, each like a loaf of bread. Center: **Porkfish** (*Anisotremus virginicus*). Often found in large schools, this yellow, black and gray fish grows to a foot. (Caribbean.)

The fish are all **Yellow Damselfish** (*Eupomacentrus planifrons*). This very hardy fish of the Caribbean is yellow with a prominent black spot when young. Above is an adult. Below is

Brain Coral (phylum Cnidaria), one of a group of hard-to-identify stony corals, in a shape like that of a brain. In the background is **Fire Coral** (see page 22).

The fish is of the species **Brown Chromis** (*Chromis multi-lineatus*), a small fish that eats plankton. Bottom, left: **Slate Pencil Urchin** (*Eucidaris tribuloides*), another species of sea urchin. In the background is the **Bushy Gorgonian** (*Plexaura flexuosa*), another coral of the odd group of Gorgonians. (Caribbean.)

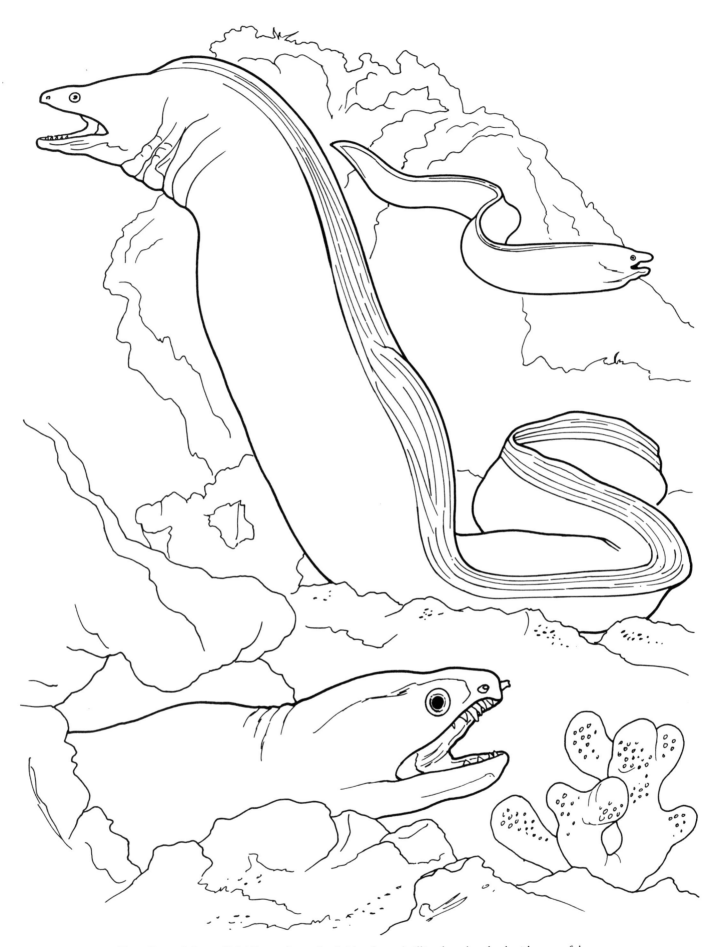

Top: **Green Moray Eel** (*Gymnothorax funebris*), a large, brilliantly colored eel with powerful jaws. Below is the **Goldentail Moray Eel** (*Muriaena miliaris*). (Caribbean.)

Swimming among a number of sponges here is the **Graysby** (*Petrometepon cruentum*), a red-spotted type of Grouper. (Caribbean.)

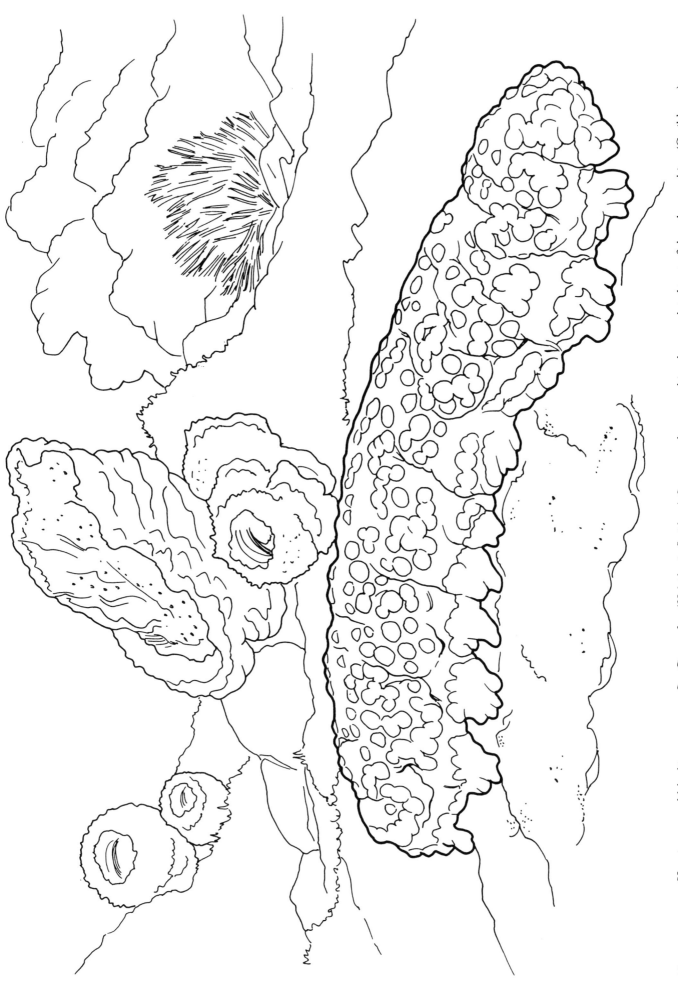

Here is a very odd-looking creature: a **Sea Cucumber** (*Holothuria floridana*). Sea cucumbers are echinoderms, related to starfish and sea urchins. (Caribbean.)

The well-known **Barracuda** (*Sphyraena* sp.). Barracuda may actually be any of several species of fierce predatory fish, growing up to six feet long. They often travel in large schools. (Caribbean.)

Spiny Puffer (*Tetraodon* sp.). Like all puffers this spiny fish puffs itself up to make life difficult for would-be predators. Bottom: before puffing; top: after puffing. (Caribbean.)

Top: the **Barred Hamlet** (*Hypoplectrus puella*). This small but voracious brown-and-white fish is related to the Groupers. It is the most common Hamlet. A much rarer member of the family (below) is the **Shy Hamlet** (*Hypoplectrus guttavarius*), a small, brilliantly colored (orange and black) fish. (Caribbean.)

All three of these fish are **Squirrelfish** (*Holocentrus ascensionis*). These large-eyed fish hide under crevices in coral and rocks and come out at night to feed. (Caribbean.)

Creole Wrasse (*Clepticus parrai*). This wrasse is a spectacularly beautiful purple or violet. Large schools of Creole Wrasses are common in the outer reefs of the Caribbean and adjoining waters. The most prominent coral in this drawing is a **Sea Fan** (*Gorgonia* sp.), a coral, one of a number of related species, with broad, branching, fanlike structures. (Caribbean.)

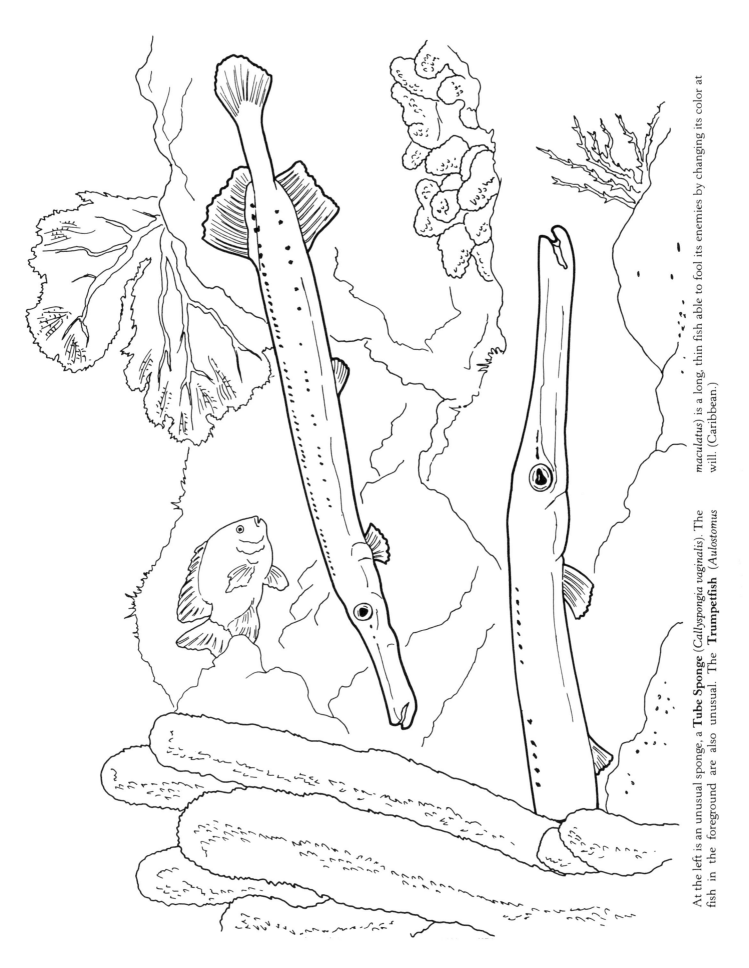

At the left is an unusual sponge, a **Tube Sponge** (*Callyspongia vaginalis*). The fish in the foreground are also unusual. The **Trumpetfish** (*Aulostomus maculatus*) is a long, thin fish able to fool its enemies by changing its color at will. (Caribbean.)

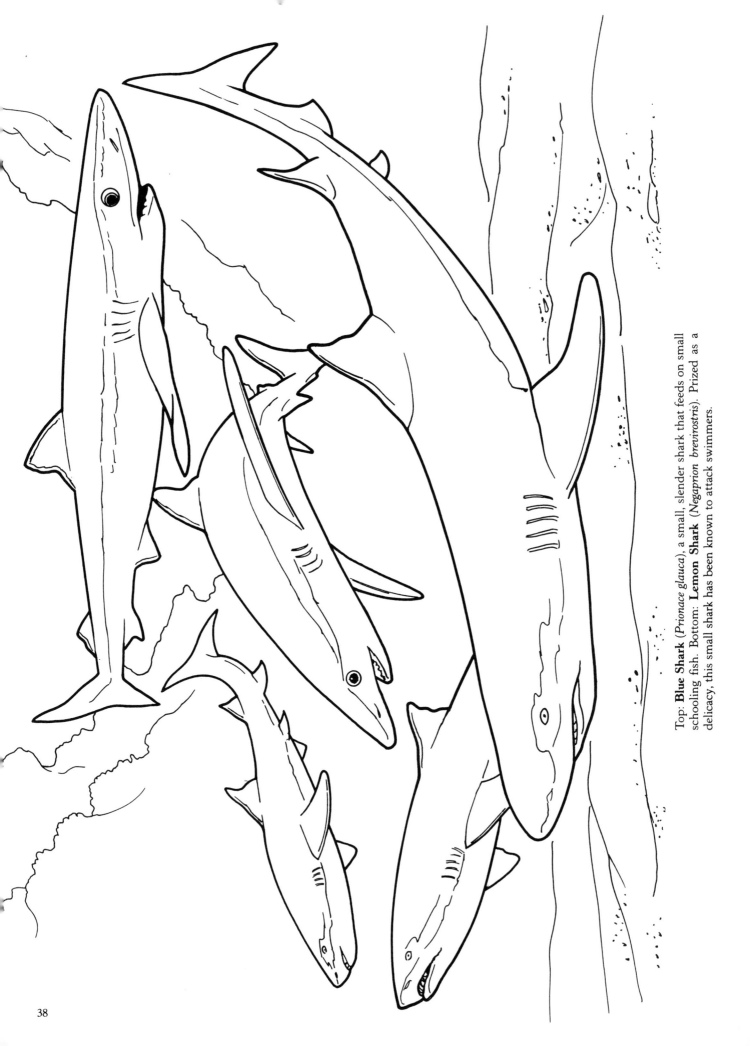

Top: **Blue Shark** (*Prionace glauca*), a small, slender shark that feeds on small schooling fish. Bottom: **Lemon Shark** (*Negaprion brevirostris*). Prized as a delicacy, this small shark has been known to attack swimmers.

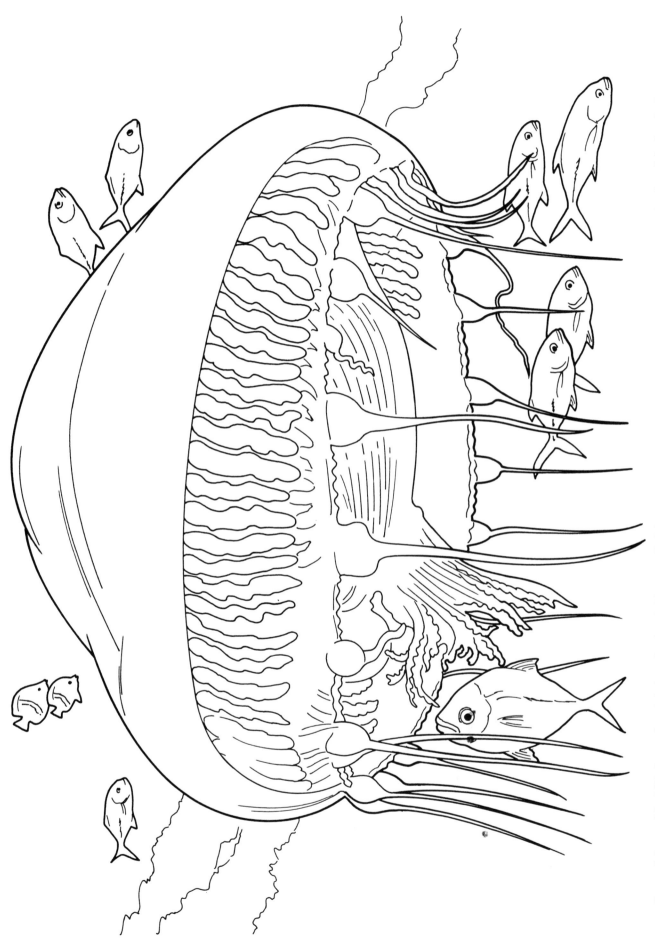

Center: **Many-ribbed Hydromedusa** (phylum Cnidaria). This is a jellyfish or polyp similar to those that build corals, except it is free-swimming. In its tentacles is a **Horse-eye Jack** (*Caranx latus*), a schooling fish that feeds on shrimp and other small creatures.

Center: **Atlantic Bottlenose Dolphin** (*Tursiops truncatus*). No sea mammal is as well known or loved as this intelligent, friendly creature, although it is better known to most people from its performances in aquarium shows than from being sighted in the wild. (Caribbean.)

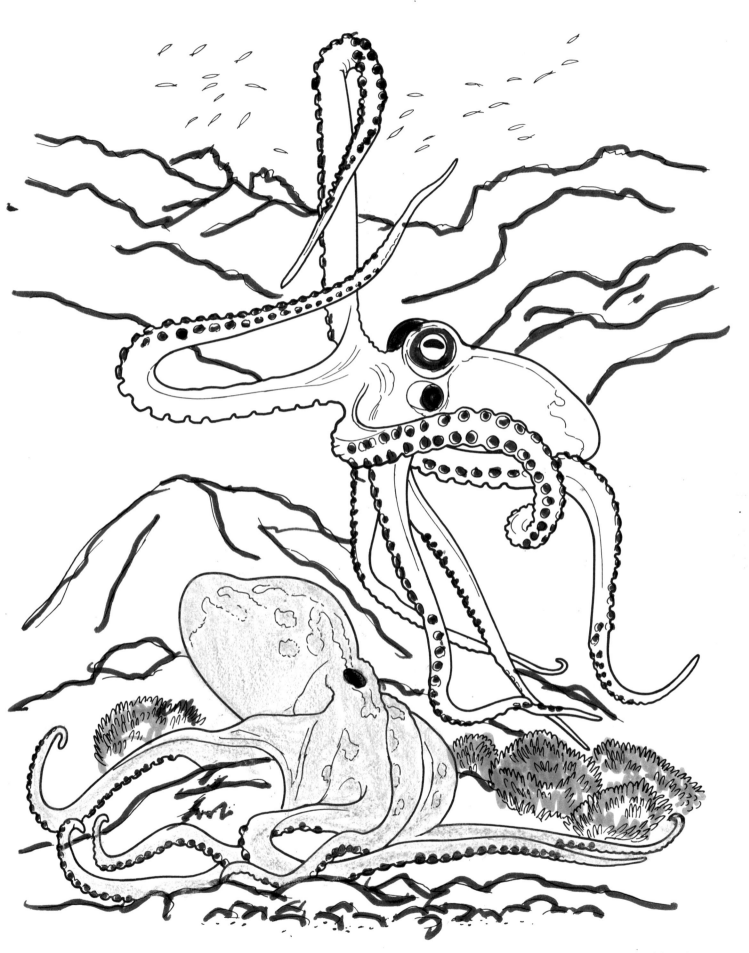

Here is a creature everyone knows: the **Octopus** (phylum Mollusca), related to the squids, clams and even snails. (Caribbean.)

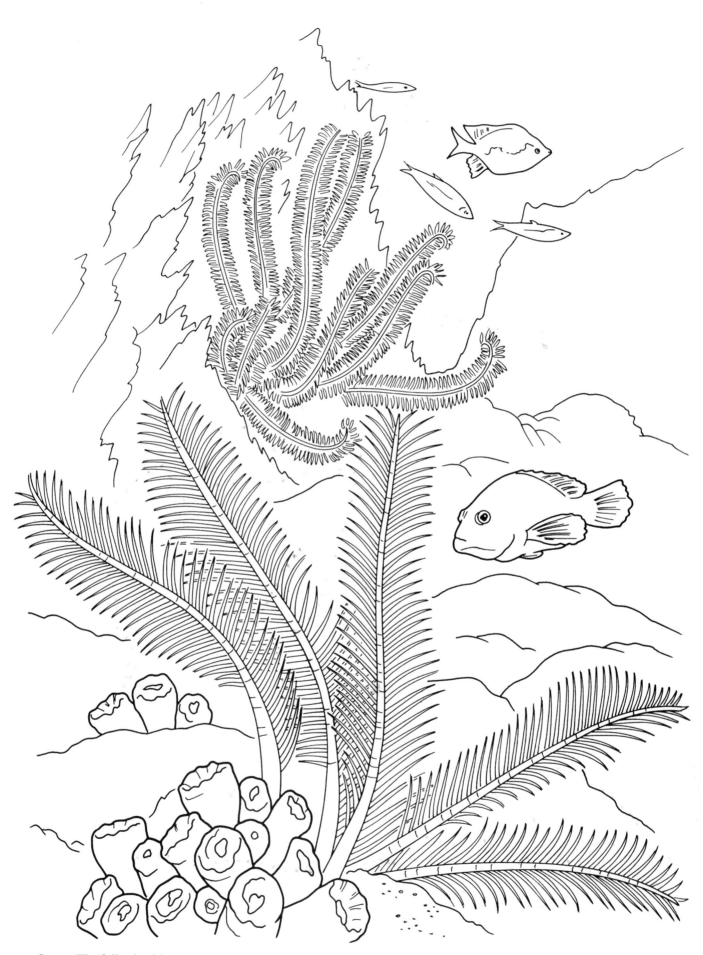

Center: The frilly plantlike creatures are Crinoids. A **Crinoid** (*Nemaster rubiginosa*) is actually a type of starfish with very thin limbs. At the bottom is **Orange Tube Coral** (*Tubastrea aurea*), a type of coral that does not build reefs. (Caribbean.)

The **Queen Angelfish** (*Holocanthus ciliaris*), stately, with a bright blue outline, is a popular aquarium fish. A juvenile swims below. In the foreground is **a Tubular Sponge** (*Verongia longissima*). (Caribbean.)

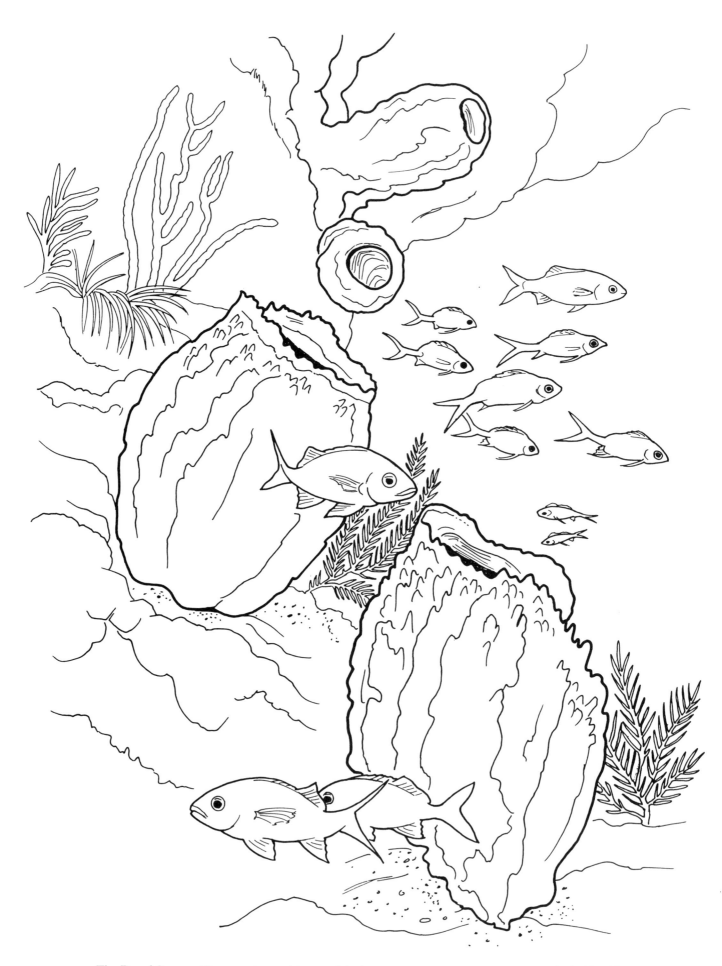

The **Barrel Sponge** (*Xestospongia muta*) is one of the largest sponges, growing to 1.5 meters high. (Caribbean.)

The **Blue-spotted Sting Ray** (*Taenuria lymna*) is a lovely member of its odd family (closely related to sharks), sometimes kept in aquariums. (Caribbean.)

Bluehead (*Thalassoma bifasciatus*). The striking blue head of this yellow wrasse is exhibited only by adult males, shown here. (Caribbean.)

Cottonwick (*Haemulon melanurum*). This small fish, related to the grunts, is seen swimming in a school through a huge reef in the Caribbean.

Alphabetical List of Common Names

Alphabetical List of Scientific Names